WORKING IN
MUSIC

by Alexis Burling

12 STORY LIBRARY

www.12StoryLibrary.com

Copyright © 2018 by 12-Story Library, Mankato, MN 56003. All rights reserved. No part of this book may be reproduced or utilized in any form or by any means without written permission from the publisher.

12-Story Library is an imprint of Bookstaves and Press Room Editions

Produced for 12-Story Library by Red Line Editorial

Photographs ©: Ronald Sumners/Shutterstock Images, cover, 1; Jstone/Shutterstock Images, 4; Christian Bertrand/Shutterstock Images, 5; Lev Radin/Shutterstock Images, 6; microgen/iStockphoto, 7; DragonImages/iStockphoto, 8; Nejron Photo/Shutterstock Images, 9; Minerva Studio/Shutterstock Images, 10; racorn/Shutterstock Images, 11; oneinchpunch/iStockphoto, 12, 28; monkeybusinessimages/iStockphoto, 13; Featureflash Photo Agency/Shutterstock Images, 14; Debby Wong/Shutterstock Images, 15; grandriver/iStockphoto, 16; track5/iStockphoto, 17; Anatolii Babii/iStockphoto, 18; Nando Machado/Shutterstock Images, 19; santypan/Shutterstock Images, 20; kenary820/Shutterstock Images, 21; Highwaystarz-Photography/iStockphoto, 22; Monkey Business Images/Shutterstock Images, 23; Miriam Doerr Martin Frommherz/Shutterstock Images, 24; SilviaJansen/iStockphoto, 25; Dziurek/Shutterstock Images, 26, 29; andresr/iStockphoto, 27

Library of Congress Cataloging-in-Publication Data
Names: Burling, Alexis.
Title: Working in music / by Alexis Burling.
Description: Mankato, MN : 12-Story Library, [2017] | Series: Career files | Includes bibliographical references and index.
Identifiers: LCCN 2016047456 (print) | LCCN 2016048066 (ebook) | ISBN 9781632354471 (hardcover : alk. paper) | ISBN 9781632355140 (pbk. : alk. paper) | ISBN 9781621435662 (hosted e-book)
Subjects: LCSH: Music trade--Vocational guidance--Juvenile literature.
Classification: LCC ML3795 .B866 2017 (print) | LCC ML3795 (ebook) | DDC 780.23--dc23
LC record available at https://lccn.loc.gov/2016047456

Printed in the United States of America
022017

Access free, up-to-date content on this topic plus a full digital version of this book. Scan the QR code on page 31 or use your school's login at 12StoryLibrary.com.

Table of Contents

What Does a Career in Music Look Like?

Imagine Selena Gomez performing in front of a sold-out audience. The strobe lights flash. Thousands of adoring fans are singing along and dancing to her music. How would it feel to be one of the world's most admired pop stars?

Being a lead singer like Gomez is thrilling. But there are other career opportunities in music that are just as exciting. Musicians land lead roles in operas and plays. Others choose technical or business types of jobs. They produce record albums or book tour dates for bands. With the right training or education, some even use music to heal illnesses.

Selena Gomez won the 2016 Teen Choice Female Artist award.

Working in music is one of the most creative career choices. It is flexible, too. Musicians often work night and weekend gigs. They also work in many environments—in a recording studio, a classroom, or even their bedrooms.

People need certain skills to work in the music industry. Practice and patience are key. Performers face a lot of rejection. Confidence is a must. But other music jobs are steadier. Music teachers receive regular paychecks. Their rewards are huge: they inspire a love of music in others.

3

Estimated percentage of job growth for musicians by the year 2024.

- Being a performer is exciting.
- Working on the technical or business side of music can be more dependable.
- Some musicians keep flexible schedules.
- Becoming a musician takes patience and skill.

People in the music industry often work nights.

The Band Takes the Spotlight

In 1964, it took six weeks for the Beatles to become one of the most famous bands in history. Today music acts such as One Direction and Fifth Harmony have millions of fans worldwide. What makes a band popular?

Successful bands are made up of several talented members who share the spotlight. Some play the bass or drums. Others sing.

Fifth Harmony started out with five members who combined their vocals into catchy tunes.

TAYLOR SWIFT: POP SUPERSTAR

Taylor Swift got her start in music before she was 10 years old. She performed at cafés in her Pennsylvania hometown. In 2004, her family moved to Nashville so she could pursue a career in music. She was 14. That same year, she signed her first record deal. In 2016, Swift became the world's top-earning celebrity, worth $170 million. She also became the first woman to win Album of the Year twice at the Grammys for her own albums.

Session musicians may work with many bands.

There are also solo artists such as Justin Bieber and Ariana Grande. They are the lead performers. They often use session musicians. These musicians are important. They can learn a song in just a few hours. Most are freelancers. They are hired to accompany bands on tour. Some fill in the background music on recordings.

Bands create albums. They sell CDs and records. Their songs are available on websites such as Spotify and Pandora. Bands may post music videos on YouTube to attract a fan base.

Most bands go on tour to promote their music. They travel to cities worldwide. They perform in local venues and huge stadiums. Some get asked to perform their best songs live on television.

700
Weeks in a row that the Beatles sold more than 1,000 copies of the album *1*.

- Bands are made up of members who sing and play instruments.
- Many musicians share their music on websites such as Spotify.
- Touring is a great way to sell records and attract fans.

Music Producers Direct the Acts

Albums are fun to listen to. But creating a record takes a lot of time. It can also be expensive.

That is where music producers come in. They are musicians' mentors. Musicians need help making recordings sound their best. Producers give bands advice. They help bands with song lyrics. They recommend session musicians.

Music producers also direct how a record gets made. They schedule time in a recording studio. They make sure deadlines are met. Some help arrange the song order on an album. Others supervise sound engineers. They tune instruments and test microphones to make sure everything works well.

A music producer must be good at math. Many manage the budget. They keep track of how many albums are sold.

Producers give artists advice on song lyrics.

16
Age of Ebony Oshunrinde when she produced a song for Jay Z.

- Music producers help musicians record albums.
- Daily tasks include scheduling time in a recording studio and keeping track of the budget.
- Math is an important skill for producers to have.

Having an ear for tone is another important skill. The best producers know how voices and instruments should work together to make the next big hit.

PHARRELL WILLIAMS: HIT PRODUCER

Pharrell Williams first attracted fans as a member of the band N.E.R.D. In 2014, his solo album *Girl* won a Grammy for Best Urban Contemporary Album. But Williams got his start as a music producer. As part of the Neptunes, he became one of the top producers in the business. His early clients included Justin Timberlake and Jay Z. In 2015, a song Williams produced won Best Rap Song of the year.

Producers often work with sound engineers.

Do Musicians Need Degrees?

There are many types of musicians. There is no one path to success. A knowledge of notes and how to play an instrument is valuable. But additional education is not always necessary.

Not all musicians attend college. As of 2016, pop star Justin Bieber only had his high school diploma. High school graduate Kelly Clarkson found fame on television. She won the first season of the television show *American Idol*. For some performers, experience makes more of a difference than schooling.

Other music jobs require certificates or degrees. Audio and video equipment technicians usually take classes for a year. Broadcast engineers earn a two-year associate's degree. Students take courses in production management and sound editing. Sound editing combines all the musical elements into a song. Students can get on-the-job training at a recording studio.

A college degree is important for the most skilled positions in music. Orchestra members attend conservatory programs, such as

Some musicians take private lessons during college.

77

Average percent of Juilliard's full-time undergraduate students who receive financial aid.

- A college degree is not required to become a musician.
- Technical musicians usually earn certificates or associate's degrees.
- Musicians trying for more skilled positions go to college.
- Conservatory programs accept only the top music students.

Juilliard. Students have to audition in order to get in. Top teachers instruct the students. Conservatory programs help musicians get jobs after graduation.

THINK ABOUT IT

Which path do you think is most effective for making a career in music: a formal music education or trying to make it big on your own?

Broadcast engineers study subjects such as math.

JUILLIARD SCHOOL

Juilliard is the top music school in the United States. It is located in New York City. Each year, approximately 5 percent of singers and 16 percent of instrumental musicians who apply get into the program. Classes are hard. Students can earn a Bachelor of Music, a Master of Music, or a Doctor of Musical Arts. Former students include jazz musician Miles Davis and cellist Yo-Yo Ma.

How Musicians Earn a Living

Earning a living in the music industry can be difficult. A musician's income is not always steady. Most are paid by the gig or by the hour. But others are hired by a company and receive a yearly salary.

According to the US Department of Labor, the average hourly rate for musicians and singers was $24.20 per hour as of May 2015. The wages are low. Some freelance musicians or technicians do not make enough money to support themselves or a family. Many get jobs in restaurants or music venues to help pay the bills.

Bands get money from each record they sell. Performers also make money from concert ticket sales and merchandise such as tour T-shirts.

Some performers have to take other jobs to supplement their income.

Teaching at a university provides a steady income.

Companies who use a band's music to promote products must also pay musicians.

A career as a performer can be hit or miss. But there are more dependable careers in music.

University music teachers earn a regular paycheck. In 2015, their salary averaged $79,180 per year. They have paid sick leave and health benefits.

$1 million

Average amount the biggest names in music make at a concert.

- Many performers are paid hourly or by the gig.
- Some musicians get other jobs to help pay the bills.
- Steadier career options include being a music teacher.

BEYONCÉ'S BOUNTY

Music is only one way Beyoncé Knowles earns her fortune. In 2010, she created her own perfume, called Heat. She has also designed clothing. In 2016, she launched Ivy Park. Full of sweatshirts, leggings, and T-shirts, the activewear brand is geared toward women on the go.

Composers Write Masterpieces

Think about the songs on the radio. Whether they are classical or rock, composers wrote each one. Composers write tunes and song lyrics. They also string melodies together to form symphonies. Some of today's famous composers are John Williams, Arvo Pärt, and Philip Glass.

Composers write music for bands and orchestras. Film studios hire them to write theme music. Kristen Anderson-Lopez and Robert Lopez won an Oscar for the song they wrote called "Let It Go" for the film *Frozen*. And composers write music for TV shows' opening credits.

A composer's average salary varies. Some earned less than $21,070 in 2015.

John Williams has composed music for many films including *Star Wars* and three Harry Potter films.

82,100

Number of jobs in the United States for conductors and composers in 2014.

- Composers write lyrics and arrange music.
- Some composers write background music for TV shows and films.
- Composers write jingles to advertise products.

TIME100

CHIVAS

Others earned more than $101,150 that same year. One of the highest-paying jobs is writing jingles for commercials. Jingle writers usually get paid by the job. They can make anywhere from $100 to $8,000 or more per commercial.

Not all composers need degrees. Pop composers do not need a degree, although many do have degrees. They get clients by sending musicians or companies demo tapes of their songs. Classical composers usually need a master's degree in music theory or music composition.

Anderson-Lopez and Lopez also took home a Grammy for "Let it Go."

Sound Engineers Master the Audio

Sound engineers are some of music's most important workers. They set up and manage electrical equipment for recording studios. They need to have an ear for music. They make sure everything that is spoken, sung, or played into a microphone sounds perfect.

Most specialize in specific areas. Some work for radio programs. They manage a sound's strength and clarity. Others use computers to make special effects for television

The sound engineer makes sure recordings sound just right.

Sound engineers learn how to run complex equipment in college.

or movies. Sound mixers edit songs that have already been recorded. They add or delete sounds or words to make new recordings.

Sound engineers have flexible jobs. They might run the soundboard for a stadium. Some sound engineers might be hired by a band to manage the sound for their concerts. Some sound engineers freelance. Some work for one TV program and then go on vacation when the crew is not filming!

Sound engineering is a hands-on job. It requires great computer skills. A high school diploma is fine for entry-level positions. But

more skilled work requires an audio engineering degree from a trade school or four-year college.

$82,670
Mean annual salary for a sound engineer job in the movie industry.

- Sound engineers make sure recordings are strong and clear.
- They can work in many industries, including radio, TV, and film.
- Computer skills are important.
- A degree is required for higher positions.

Record Labels Publish Music

Record labels are the music industry's publishing companies. They make the decisions for music sales and distribution. They decide which musicians to represent. They choose how much to promote a musician. This determines who becomes famous. Labels also choose which songs are played on the radio. They pick which stations play those songs. They set a record's release date.

Record labels can be helpful for new musicians. Some have staff to schedule media interviews. Marketing managers come up with creative ways to promote albums. Other people handle a band's finances while they are on tour.

Before the Internet, musicians needed to sign with a record label. That is how they made it big. But that has changed. In 2016, there were only three major labels left:

One way record labels promote artists is through online platforms.

iTunes

The Beatles. Now on iTunes.

$15 billion

Amount of global recorded music sales in 2015.

- Record labels help musicians promote and sell records.
- Some musicians start their own labels to control their own careers.
- There are three major labels: Universal, Sony, and Warner.

SHAWN MENDES: FAME FIRST

Before the year 2000, most musicians got famous by signing with a record label. But Canadian Shawn Mendes became famous without a record label. In August 2013, the 15-year-old made a clip of himself singing a Justin Bieber song. He uploaded it to the video-sharing service Vine. The next day, he had 10,000 followers. By October, he had 200,000. Then Island Records gave Mendes his first record deal in June 2014.

Universal Music Group, Sony BMG, and Warner Music Group.

Many musicians do not like that record labels have so much control. Some launch their own companies so they have control. Prince quit Warner Brothers in 1994 and created NPG Records. Jay Z formed Roc Nation in 2008.

Universal Music Group owns 91 smaller labels.

UNIVERSAL

UNIVERSAL MUSIC UK
UNIVERSAL MUSIC GROUP INTERNATIONAL

364 - 366 KENSINGTON HIGH STREET

How Technology Has Changed Music

In the past, music lovers went to a record store. They bought a record, cassette tape, or CD. They listened to songs on their stereos or in their cars. But this has changed over the past 20 years.

Musicians can now mix and record albums digitally from their own computers. Software such as GarageBand and Ardour make laying down tracks simpler. Then musicians can put songs on the Internet for anyone to find.

Today it is much easier for musicians to record music in their own homes.

45

Percent of global music industry income driven by digital sales in 2016.

- Today people listen to digital music files.
- Musicians can create albums using computer software.
- Social media helps musicians gain fans.
- Consumers can find new music through streaming sites.

THINK ABOUT IT

Do you think technology has helped the music industry? Why or why not? How is technology shaping the music of the future?

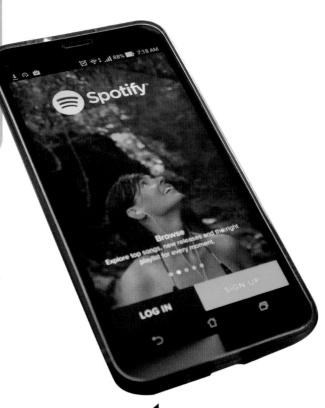

Technology has made it easier for new artists to get discovered. A new musician can gain a huge following by using social media. They do not even need to leave their hometowns. Websites such as YouTube are great for posting music videos. Fans can then share the videos on their own social media sites.

Streaming services such as Spotify, SoundCloud, and Tidal have also changed the industry. They allow users to listen to music for free or for a low monthly cost. The musicians do not make much money this way. But the exposure is worth it for many budding artists.

Users can listen to music for free on Spotify.

21

Music Teachers Inspire

One of the most rewarding types of jobs for musicians is teaching others how to sing or play an instrument. Music instructors have many career options. They can take full-time or part-time jobs. They can teach students at any level. Some work in kindergarten classrooms. Others work on college campuses.

Still others lead marching bands or become choir directors.

Many music teachers run their own businesses. They have private clients. They give lessons out of their homes. Depending on the instrument, some teachers rent studios to keep the noise down

Some music teachers direct school choirs.

in their neighborhoods. These instructors are usually paid by the hour or per session. Those who work for a school or organization have steadier pay.

The path to becoming a music teacher is fairly simple. Those who teach in public school need a bachelor's degree in music education. They might also need a teaching license, depending on state requirements. University music professors usually have a master's degree. They major in whichever field of music interests them most.

This music teacher gives private lessons.

$54,550
Average annual salary for an elementary school music teacher in the United States.

- Music teachers can teach full- or part-time.
- Private tutors get paid by the hour or per session.
- Elementary school teachers need a bachelor's degree.
- Most music professors have master's degrees.

Private music teachers need to be good at what they teach. They should have training through private lessons or a music school. Some already have full-time careers in other areas. They tutor students part-time.

Music Therapists Heal

Listening to music can affect emotions. An Adele tune might remind a girl of her best friend at summer camp. A Wiz Khalifa song might spark memories of playing hoops with neighborhood pals. Music can make people happy. It can also heal pain.

Some therapists use music to treat illnesses such as anxiety or depression. They give music lessons. They help clients write song lyrics to improve the clients' moods. Other therapists work with people who have brain injuries. Singing aloud sometimes helps improve mental development.

Music therapists bring joy to many people's lives.

Music therapists work in many settings. Those treating patients with drug addiction might work in an addiction recovery center. Other music therapists have offices in schools or retirement homes. Music therapists partner with doctors, psychologists, or physical therapists. They give clients the best care possible.

Music therapy offers a steady income. Some jobs pay $76,800 or more per year. But this career requires a lot of education. Therapists need a bachelor's degree. They usually get a music therapy degree. They must find a school that offers the program.

480
Minimum number of on-the-job hours required to become a music therapist.

- Music can help treat illnesses.
- Music therapists use singing, songwriting, and song listening in treatment.
- Music therapists need a bachelor's degree.

Many also get a master's degree. Music therapy students also get on-the-job training at hospitals or health clinics.

Music therapy helps people relax.

Is a Career in Music Right for You?

There are challenges and rewards to a career in music. And there are lots of options to consider. Every path is different.

Many musicians have some general traits in common. Every musician should have talent. A talent may be playing one or several instruments well. It may be teaching someone else to sing. Often the most talented musicians are rewarded with fame or a steady income.

Discipline is also key to success. Musicians and vocalists need to take lessons. They need to practice every day. Sound engineers or musicians who want to record their own music need technical skills. They need to master the computer programs and digital equipment required to record or broadcast music.

Those in the music industry should also be comfortable working around people. Being outgoing is useful

Music careers are competitive, so talent and hard work are important.

Being good with computers is an important skill to have in the music industry.

when performing or searching for new clients. A positive attitude also helps. All jobs in the music field are competitive. Staying optimistic after a rejection can make all the difference.

Lastly, creativity, an ear for tone, and knowing math are important in most music careers. Math is useful for musicians who want to manage their own money. It is also useful for the more technical jobs such as sound engineering.

92
Percent of millennials in the United States who listen to the radio every week.

- Becoming a musician takes talent.
- An outgoing personality is helpful for performers and producers.
- Musicians should practice every day.
- Math is useful for many music careers.

THINK ABOUT IT

Do you think becoming a musician is a good career choice for you? Why or why not? Which type of specialty or focus do you think fits your personality best?

Conductor

Description: Direct the way members of an orchestra or other musical group play their instruments during live performances and recordings; select songs to be performed; manage rehearsals
Training/Education: Bachelor's or master's degree in music theory, music composition, or conducting
Outlook: Rising
Average salary: $49,820

Musical Instrument Repairer and Tuner

Description: Fix percussion, stringed, reed, or wind instruments; many pick one specialty, such as piano tuning
Training/Education: Optional degree from a trade school; prior on-the-job training
Outlook: Rising
Average salary: $35,660

Music Publicist

Description: Promote musicians through social media; write press releases; book interviews with the press
Training/Education: Bachelor's degree in public relations, journalism, communications, English, or business
Outlook: Rising
Average Salary: $56,770

Radio DJ

Description: Curate music for radio shows; announce songs played during a show; interview musicians as guests
Training/Education: Bachelor's degree in journalism, broadcasting, or communications; prior on-the-job work experience at college or professional radio station
Outlook: In decline
Average Salary: $30,080

Glossary

budget
A plan for making and spending money.

conservatory
A college where students can study music or art.

demo tapes
Recordings that show off a musician's talent.

discipline
Dedication and willingness to work.

freelancers
People who work for themselves or more than one company.

gigs
Concerts, performances, jobs.

jingles
Songs used to promote products.

soundboard
Equipment used in concerts to regulate sounds and instruments.

symphonies
Long musical compositions played by orchestras.

tone
An instrument or voice's quality of sound.

For More Information

Books

Guillain, Charlotte. *Music*. Chicago, IL: Heinemann, 2013.

Hopper, Jessica. *The Girls' Guide to Rocking: How to Start a Band, Book Gigs, and Get Rolling to Rock Stardom*. New York: Workman Publishing, 2009.

Morreale, Marie. *Taylor Swift: Born to Sing!* New York: Children's Press, 2017.

Visit 12StoryLibrary.com

Scan the code or use your school's login at **12StoryLibrary.com** for recent updates about this topic and a full digital version of this book. Enjoy free access to:

- Digital ebook
- Breaking news updates
- Live content feeds
- Videos, interactive maps, and graphics
- Additional web resources

Note to educators: Visit 12StoryLibrary.com/register to sign up for free premium website access. Enjoy live content plus a full digital version of every 12-Story Library book you own for every student at your school.

Index

About the Author

Alexis Burling makes her living as a writer and book critic. She has written dozens of articles and books for young readers on a variety of topics ranging from current events and famous people, nutrition and fitness, relationships and career advice.

READ MORE FROM 12-STORY LIBRARY

Every 12-Story Library book is available in many formats. For more information, visit 12StoryLibrary.com.